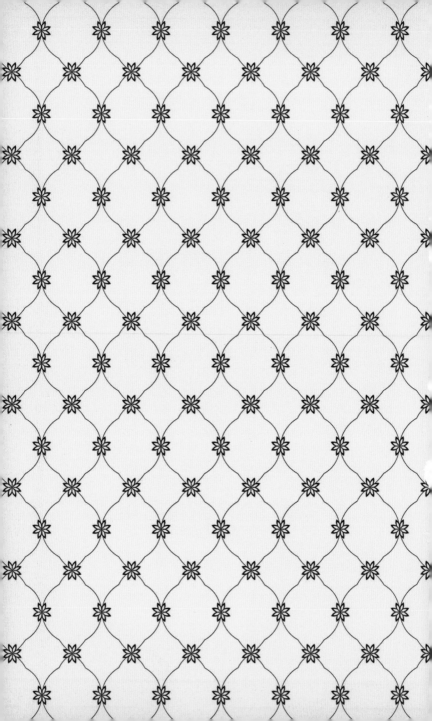

To
Hannah

From
Morgan

Your Word Is A LAMP Unto My Feet

60 DEVOTIONS

Ellie Claire® Gift & Paper Expressions
Franklin, TN 37067
EllieClaire.com
Ellie Claire is a registered trademark of Worthy Media, Inc.

Your Word Is a Lamp devotional
© 2018 by Ellie Claire
Published by Ellie Claire, an imprint of Worthy Publishing Group, a division
of Worthy Media, Inc.

ISBN 978-1-63326-204-1

Stock or custom editions of Ellie Claire titles may be purchased in bulk
for educational, business, ministry, fundraising, or sales promotional use.
For information, please e-mail info@EllieClaire.com.

Illustration by Diana Nguyen
Cover design by Melissa Reagan
Interior design and layout by Bart Dawson

Printed in China

1 2 3 4 5 6 7 8 9 – HaHa – 22 21 20 19 18

To You, O LORD, I lift up my soul.

O my God, I trust in You;...

Show me Your ways, O LORD;

Teach me Your paths.

PSALM 25:1–2, 4 NKJV

A Beautiful Reflection

*When God created human beings,
he made them to be like himself.*

GENESIS 5:1 NLT

"Mirror, mirror on the wall, I'm more than my appearance, after all." Do you believe that? Or does the mirror play a larger part than you would like in your self-image? Television, movies, and modern culture try to convince you that image is everything, that youth, killer abs, and maintaining the same weight as a preteen girl are not only desirable, but expected.

God disagrees. His Word tells us our image is a reflection of His own. But you can't see this kind of image in the mirror. God is spirit, something you can't see. It's true, Jesus walked this earth dressed in a human body for a time. But God's image isn't even found in the face of Christ. God's image is more like a picture of His heart.

You were created in that image, created to reflect love, mercy, forgiveness, and grace. You'll never find these in your bathroom mirror. Instead, believe and confess what His Word says about you, then look at the reflection your life casts on those around you. That's where God's image can most clearly be seen. Seeking that image is the first step on the path of true beauty.

Light for your path

1 Samuel 16:7
Psalm 139:16
John 6:37
Romans 12:3, 6
Ephesians 1:5; 3:20

His love lifts us to a higher beauty.

ANONYMOUS

You have a Creator who has formed you to think,
love, speak, play, feel, see, smell, and taste, just like Him.
There is no other creature on earth like you.

JENNIFER GERELDS

Remember Me

*Then God remembered Rachel; he listened
to her and enabled her to conceive.*

GENESIS 30:22 NIV

*A*rchimedes is considered one of the greatest scientists and mathematicians in world history. But apparently the scholar from Greece was also an absentminded genius. When the Romans invaded Greece, a Roman soldier was ordered to bring Archimedes before the emperor. Lost in deep thought, Archimedes kept tracing an important problem in the dust while the soldier kept tapping on the intellect's shoulder. He didn't pay attention even after the frustrated soldier drew his sword.

Sometimes in the more pressing moments of life it can feel as if God is absentminded too. You keep tapping on His shoulder, but He seems distracted by some other problem. Sometimes it can feel as if God has passed you over and moved on to more urgent affairs of the universe.

But the truth is, the Creator, who knows the complexities of every individual who has ever lived, always remembers you. By His Word, we know that He always was; He created time as we know it. He is truly ancient, but never forgetful. He recalls and cares about every detail in your days, right down to that scratch on your arm and the words you'll speak today. He will not overlook a single second of your day. Nothing fades from God's memory—especially not a beloved child like you.

Light for your path

Deuteronomy 1:30; 33:27
Psalm 3:3; 91:7; 94:18; 125:2
Isaiah 43:2; 52:12
John 10:27–29

God walks with us.
He scoops us up in His arms
or simply sits with us in silent strength
until we cannot avoid
the awesome recognition
that yes, even now, He is here.

GLORIA GAITHER

Our Own Story

I, the LORD, am your healer.

EXODUS 15:26 NASB

Whenever we receive exciting news, the first thing we want to do is pass it on! All we have to do is tell a few friends, and soon everyone has heard all about it.

News traveled quickly in Jesus's time, too, even though there were no phones and certainly no e-mail—only a word from one person to the next. No sooner had the Lord healed a person in one town than a crowd from the next town poured out to meet Him, and with each healing, the crowds grew larger and larger. What to some was a blessing, and to others a spectacle, Jesus's healing miracles reflected God's desire and ability to heal. His Word is full of examples of His power and desire to heal individuals.

Though He often also works through physicians, surgeons, and counselors to treat our wounds of body and mind, there are some wounds too deep inside the heart for anyone to reach. These are the wounds God soothes with His presence and eases with Spirit-sent gifts of patience, faith, and hope. Though a heart-deep wound may yet leave a scar, with Him a scar can serve as the foundation for serenity, a closer relationship with the Restorer of our soul, and the beautiful story of how He changed us forever.

Light for your path

Exodus 23:25
Psalm 30:2; 41:3; 91:3–10;
103:2–5; 107:20
Proverbs 4:20–22
Isaiah 53:5
Jeremiah 17:14; 30:17; 33:6
Matthew 4:23; 9:35
Mark 16:17–18
Luke 6:19
Romans 8:11
James 1:6; 5:13–16
3 John 2

When we dare to speak the truth
of our stories, it is an act of war
against the enemies of our hearts....
When we speak the truth about our stories,
we set each other free.

HOLLEY GERTH

Learning to Count

*And He said, "My Presence will
go with you, and I will give you rest."*
EXODUS 33:14 NKJV

Sometimes we count the wrong things, like how much money is in the bank or how many bills are on the table. Don't misunderstand. We should be responsible and manage our money well. But all of us go through seasons in life when our best plans, our best efforts, our best intentions fall short. That shortfall might be felt in our wallets, in our health, in our relationships.

Jesus counted five loaves and two small fish and judged that He had enough to feed five thousand. Maybe you have been the recipient of a miracle of faith. You know there are some things that simply cannot be explained. On paper, it looked like it would never work. But it did. Money showed up in the mailbox. The phone call you didn't expect came. The doctor's report came back, and the tumor was gone. You don't know how these things happened, but they did—and they still do!

When your assets grow thin and your troubles are adding up, it's time to run to the One who counts a little differently than you do, and believe what His Word says. It's time to find shelter in His presence and let Him do the math.

Let Him teach you that one plus God is much more than enough.

Light for your path

Deuteronomy 28:8, 12
Matthew 6:33; 21:22
2 Corinthians 9:8
Philippians 4:19
Hebrews 4:15–16; 10:19–20
1 Peter 4:10–11

Never yield to gloomy anticipation.
Place your hope and confidence in God.
He has no record of failure.

L. B. COWMAN

Heard It through the Grapevine

Do not go about spreading slander among your people.

LEVITICUS 19:16 NIV

Like grapes, women often hang out in bunches. We cluster together, waiting to hear something juicy. We chat about the latest office news, parenting tips, beauty secrets, or anything else that crosses our minds. Companionship like this can be a wonderful thing, as long as we strive to bring out the best in each other. But it's easy for the latest "news" to deteriorate into the latest "gossip."

Gossip brings out the worst, not the best, in us. It's telling a story that isn't ours to tell, often when we don't know all the facts. Once it's out of our mouths, gossip spreads like a fungus through our relational vine. Even if it's not intentionally malicious, it can wind up causing damage to reputations, relationships, and hearts—not the least of which is our own. Love speaks well of others. Gossip enjoys being the center of attention, with little regard for the truth. Which type of words would you like others speaking about you?

God's Word is full of instruction on the importance of guarding our tongue. Let's give away the kind of words we'd like most to receive.

Light for your path

Joshua 1:8
Psalm 19:14; 119:11, 105
Proverbs 16:23; 18:21
Matthew 12:34
Romans 10:8–10
Hebrews 4:12

*No one else's poor choice of words
can dictate the way you choose to walk.*

ANN VOSKAMP

*To be candid without ostentation or design—
to take the good of everybody's character
and make it still better, and say nothing
of the bad—belongs to you alone.*

JANE AUSTEN

God's Great Heart

The LORD bless you and keep you;
the LORD make His face shine
upon you, and be gracious to you;
the LORD lift up His countenance
upon you, and give you peace.

NUMBERS 6:24–26 NKJV

God's Word gives us a clear picture of the generous heart of God to bless. It is His greatest joy to give lavishly and generously to those whom He loves—and His love is indiscriminate. Are you receptive to God's blessing, aware that in an obedient relationship with God you are also in a position to experience His abundance?

God cares for you. Even concerning the smallest details of your day, it matters to the Lord that things are well with you. Did you know that He is with you to bless you when things go wrong, as well as when things go right?

God gives peace. Though this world is a troubled place, the Lord provides the calm that allows you to pillow your head at night, confident that you'll arise in the morning.

Do you trust Him when your peace is disturbed? God is attentive to you. He doesn't miss anything. Are you reciprocally attentive to Him? God prospers you. He rewards and applauds your efforts. Do you return thanks? God smiles on you. Observant and always looking for the best in you, God looks for reasons to rejoice over you. Did you know that you bless His heart with joy?

Light for your path

Joshua 1:9
Psalm 18:29–33
Isaiah 41:10; 43:2–3; 50:7
Acts 4:13–31
Romans 8:31
Ephesians 6:10–18
Philippians 4:13

When we reach the end of our strength,
wisdom, and personal resources,
we enter into the beginning
of His glorious provisions.

PATSY CLAIRMONT

God's written Word
is the plumb line for our lives
as we walk daily with him.

HENRY T. BLACKABY

On the Job

*For the LORD your God has blessed you
in everything you have done.*

DEUTERONOMY 2:7 NLT

The phrase "labor force" doesn't paint a particularly pleasant picture for women. Anything involving labor sounds painful and exhausting. But if you receive a paycheck, this force includes you. If you're a stay-at-home mom, you may not officially be part of the force, but that doesn't mean you don't labor right along with the rest of us. God didn't design work as drudgery or a pastime to keep us occupied until we're home in heaven. God intended work as a gift with a purpose.

In the Bible we read about those who built God's temple. Some were assigned jobs as singers, others as artisans. There were carpenters, goldsmiths, musicians, and priests. Everyone's job was important. They were all working in line with their individual skills and talents.

Not every job you do will utilize all of your skills. But every job will offer you the opportunity to work hard at doing something well. When you do this, you'll have something in common with those who built the temple. What you do will honor God.

Light for your path

Nehemiah 1:11
Proverbs 3:5–6
Ecclesiastes 9:10
Matthew 16:26
1 Corinthians 3:13–14
Ephesians 4:1–3
2 John 1:8

*I believe that each of us has
God-given talents within us
waiting to be brought to fruition.*

MARY KAY ASH

*Many Christian women struggle with
the I'm-not-good-enough-smart-enough-
talented-enough syndrome....
Every daughter of the King has been
uniquely designed and equipped for a purpose.*

SUSAN HUNT

Greater Trust, Fewer Fears

*Be strong and courageous, do not be afraid
or tremble at them, for the LORD
your God is the one who goes with you.
He will not fail you or forsake you.*

DEUTERONOMY 31:6 NASB

Do you fully realize that in His Word, God promises to always be with you, and He proclaims Himself trustworthy? You can always trust Him. One evidence of your faith in God is the extent to which you've handed over your fears to Him. The more you trust Him, the fewer fears you should have.

Maybe you're still riddled with fear. What can you do about it? How can you learn to trust God more? When it comes to trust, your relationship with God isn't all that different from your relationship with a close friend or spouse. Early on in a friendship, you share information about yourself a little bit at a time. As you learn to trust the other person more, you share deeper thoughts and intimate secrets, knowing your friend will carefully guard them.

One way to develop a greater trust in God and allow Him to allay your fears is to immerse yourself in His Word, particularly those passages that reassure you of His constant presence with you, His protection over you, and His care for you at all times and in every circumstance. The biblical truth about God's concern for you is your greatest and most effective weapon against the fears that plague you.

Light for your path

Psalm 23:4–5; 27:1, 5; 34:4;
56:1–13; 91:1–16
Isaiah 35:4; 41:10
John 14:27
Romans 8:15, 31, 35–39
2 Timothy 1:7
Hebrews 13:6
1 John 4:18

Courage comes from a heart
that is convinced it is loved.

BETH MOORE

Leaving the Door Open

Let the sun stand still!
JOSHUA 10:12 TLB

Throughout the Bible, we read story after story of great miracles that God performed. At first glance, it would seem like God performed these wonders for the best of the best, the most righteous men and women of the ages. But upon closer examination, we discover this isn't necessarily the case. God made the sun stand still for hours to protect Joshua's troops as they fought off attacking armies. God sent bread from heaven to a community of people who frequently complained about Him. A young man who fell asleep in church, resulting in a fatal fall from a third-story window, was raised from the dead. An argumentative fisherman hauled an impossible supply of fish from the water. And the list goes on.

All of this arms us with hope. God can come through for us, even though we know that we are far from perfect. What can God do for you? Anything! There are no limitations on the power of God. As you spend time in His presence, leave the door open for your supernatural God to show up with a solution to your impossible challenges.

Light for your path

Psalm 40:5
John 2:11; 12:37; 14:12
Acts 8:13
1 Corinthians 12:10
Galatians 3:5
Hebrews 2:4

I believe that God
is in the miracle business—
that His favorite way of working
is to pick up where our human abilities
and understandings leave off,
and then do something so wondrous
and unexpected that there's no doubt
who the God is around here.

EMILIE BARNES

The Power of God

> *Gideon said to Him, "O my lord, if the LORD is with us, why then has all this happened to us? And where are all His miracles which our fathers told us about?"*
>
> JUDGES 6:13 NKJV

The trouble with trouble is that it brings up so many things we try to keep pushed down, far away from the "nice zone." When difficult things still happen to us after we've tried to follow all of God's ways, we might wonder, *Does Christianity work? If the Lord is truly with me, why is all this happening to me?* This is a variation on the question, *Where is God when it hurts?*

The real underlying question is, *If God is all-powerful, why doesn't He just make this go away?* It's disturbing to think that He is watching our mess and seemingly choosing to let us squirm. What happened to all those stories of miracles we heard in Sunday school? Were those just fairy tales? If they *were* real, where's the power today?

God's Word shows that He doesn't flinch at our honest questions. He is always ready for real interaction with His people. And getting real with God often leads to a release of His power. He is right there in your trouble, fighting for your freedom. The question "Where's the power?" can precede the declaration, "Wow, God, You're amazing!" An honest ownership of your scariest questions can lead to a breakthrough.

Light for your path

John 6:37; 10:27–29
Philippians 1:6
2 Timothy 1:12
Hebrews 11:6; 12:2
1 John 5:13

For Christians who believe
God's promises, the future is actually
too bright to comprehend.

MARIE T. FREEMAN

You are mighty, Lord, you are mighty.
Nothing compares to you in power.
No one can equal the strength of your hand.

MARY MORRISON SUGGS

Hiding Places

Behold, he is hiding himself
by the baggage.

1 Samuel 10:22 nasb

All of us hide. All of us have said things, done things, and thought things that we don't want others to know about. We would rather forget these things ever happened. Most of us have had things done to us that we don't want to remember. Driven by shame or guilt or fear, we hide. We hide from one another. We hide from ourselves. And we try to hide from God.

But God knows all our hiding places. God alone knows all of our hidden hurts and faults. He knows our most embarrassing moments. He knows all about the things that are so painful to think about that we hide them even from ourselves.

This is why, even long after we have come to faith in Christ, Jesus is still knocking at the doors inside our soul. He's inviting us to come out of hiding and share our deepest secrets with Him. Why would He do that? Does He delight in exposing our faults? Nothing could be further from the truth! Rather, He is gently showing us that He can be trusted with our darkest secrets. He is inviting us to discover the healing and transforming power of His presence in our places of pain.

Light for your path

Psalm 90:8
Proverbs 28:13
Matthew 6:5; 23:28
Galatians 2:14
James 3:17
Revelation 2:4–5

It's not really important when
I choose to meet God every day.
What really matters is that
I show up regularly. . . . Consistency,
after all, doesn't mean perfection;
it simply means refusing to give up.

JOANNA WEAVER

Refills from God

*Jonathan went to find David
and encouraged him to stay strong
in his faith in God.*

1 Samuel 23:16 nlt

*S*ome days it doesn't take much to push your physical, emotional, and spiritual tanks toward empty. A fussy child, a displeased boss, a short-tempered spouse, and your own critical self-talk leave you feeling drained. You know the drill. Demands and interruptions squeeze out your enthusiasm, and you wilt in exhaustion.

The good thing is: None of this surprises God. He knows everything that crosses your path each day, and He knows just how much pressure and fatigue you can handle. One of the wonderful joys in following Him is that He knows just when and how to refill your tank. A stockpile of encouragement and perspective may come in the form of a loving friend who offers a hand and an understanding heart, or laughter via a well-timed greeting card may erase your weariness.

God continually surprises His children with everyday boosters. A surefire way to find strength before you enter the thick of each day is to set aside some quiet moments alone in His Word, talking to God, and listening for His voice. As your loving Provider, He is eager to sustain you no matter what you'll face. What comfort it is to know that His "service station" is open 24/7.

Light for your path

Psalm 27:5–6, 13–14; 30:5; 31:24
Matthew 11:28–30
John 14:1, 27
Romans 8:28
2 Corinthians 4:8–9, 16–18
Galatians 6:9
Philippians 1:6; 4:6–7, 19
1 Thessalonians 3:3
Hebrews 10:35–36
1 Peter 1:6–9

The Lord's chief desire is to reveal
Himself to you.... The Lord gives you
the experience of enjoying His presence.
He touches you, and His touch
is so delightful that, more than ever,
you are drawn inwardly to Him.

MADAME JEANNE GUYON

✿ 31 ✿

God...will never speak
to us through our circumstances
in a way that contradicts
His written Word.
The Bible should be our first
source of information when trying
to discern the voice of God.

RON EDMONDSON

Loved by God

*David returned home to bless
his own family.*

2 SAMUEL 6:20 NLT

Where do we find the capacity to bless those closest to us? How do we find the ability to speak life-giving words of hope and encouragement to those around us? What needs to happen in us so that our actions nurture those in our circle of influence? In a sense, the answer is simple: You can't pour water from an empty pitcher. We need to find "the blessing" ourselves. We need to be filled up to overflowing inside before we can pour affirming love out on others.

Some of us are fortunate enough to have real or surrogate parents who communicated to us, "I love you just as you are. I believe in you. You matter." Some of us are not that fortunate. But, ultimately, for all of us, our "blessing" and affirmation comes from God Himself. This is why it is so important that you let yourself be loved by God.

Linger in His Word and His presence, and let Him share with you the joy He feels that you are you. Drink in the love of God. From that place, you will be empowered to go into your world and touch people with the life-changing presence and love of Christ.

Light for your path

Proverbs 10:12
John 15:9–12
Romans 8:38–39
1 Corinthians 13:4–8, 13
Ephesians 3:16–19
1 John 4:18

I have wondered and stood amazed
that God should make a conquest
of all within me by love.

LADY HUNTINGTON

Let us use texts of scripture as fuel for our heart's fire…;
let us attend sermons, but above all,
let us be much alone with Jesus.

CHARLES H. SPURGEON

One Thing after Another

Isn't this Bathsheba...
wife of Uriah the Hittite?
2 SAMUEL 11:3 NET

From the very first chapters of God's Word, we see that God honors us with the freedom of choice. He desires to walk with us, and to be chosen above everything else in our lives. If we're not carefully guarding our path, our hearts will veer from Him, subtly at first, but ultimately leading us to places we never planned on going.

Take King David, for example. The king was at first attracted to, then lustful of, and finally had to "have" Bathsheba. He didn't plan any of the next steps—pregnancy, murder, and pain.

Sin has a way of doing that. You make one little choice (a bad one) and try to cover it up or even ignore it, and you end up getting caught in a bigger sin. How would David's life have been different if, after the first sin (the obsession with Bathsheba), he had drawn near to God, confessed his sin, and accepted the consequences?

Shine a light on your life. If you have made bad choices that have led to sin, stop the cycle before it becomes a habit. Live differently from that part of King David's story and do not let one sin turn into several. Choose to walk closely with God daily.

Light for your path

Deuteronomy 30:15–20
Joshua 24:15
2 Samuel 11:2–5
Job 34:4
Psalm 25:12; 119:30, 173
Hebrews 11:13–16
James 1:5–8

*Every choice you make
has an end result.*

ZIG ZIGLAR

*What happens outwardly in your life
is not as important as what happens inside you.
Your circumstances are temporary,
but your character will last forever.*

RICK WARREN

When God Speaks

*After the fire there was the sound
of a gentle whisper.*

1 KINGS 19:12 NLT

Have you ever had trouble hearing God's voice? It's not surprising if your answer is yes. The clatter of the world around you, as well as the clamor of your own thoughts, can muffle the clear, unmistakable sound of God speaking to you.

Once, the biblical prophet Elijah was deeply discouraged. Only after Elijah stilled the tumult of his emotions, however, could he hear God speak. In the silence of his soul, God's voice came as gently as a whisper, as tenderly as a kiss. In the stillness of his spirit, God's renewing, encouraging, and life-giving words restored him.

Today, God speaks to you softly, with gentleness and compassion. In the stillness of your spirit, He whispers words of strength and assurance. In the quietness of your soul, He murmurs expressions of love and affection.

You won't have trouble hearing His voice when your mind—and ear—is turned to Him. And with inner distractions gone, you will have the bonus of also hearing the voices of those around you speaking His Word to you.

Light for your path

1 Kings 19:11–12
Psalm 25:12; 32:8; 73:23
Proverbs 1:33; 6:22
Isaiah 30:21
Jeremiah 29:11; 33:3
John 6:63; 10:27; 16:13
Hebrews 4:7

I always begin my prayers in silence,
for it is in the silence of the heart
that God speaks.

MOTHER TERESA

Deepest communion with God is beyond words,
on the other side of silence.

MADELEINE L'ENGLE

The Uniqueness of God

*There is no one like you, LORD,
and there is no God but you.*

1 CHRONICLES 17:20 NIV

What do you consider your most distinguishing characteristic? Would it be your dimples? Or is it your naturally curly hair? Maybe you would say that your uniqueness is more of an internal issue as opposed to something physical. So, for instance, your distinctiveness might be your ability to draw a complete stranger into an intimate conversation.

Have you ever considered the uniqueness of the God whom Jesus called "Father," the One who the kings of ancient Israel called "Lord"? Have you ever pondered how distinctly different are those who diligently follow this God? The most distinguishing characteristic of God is love, which includes every expression of love that occurs within the context of a relationship: grace, gentleness, mercy, understanding, kindness, joy, and affection. He is the God who tenderly watches over the weak, who bends from His lofty dwelling place to live among the helpless, who hurries to forgive and rushes to rescue people from their self-imposed despair. Is that what you think of when you think of God? Love is His distinguishing characteristic, and as His child, you will grow to resemble Him. The more you know Him, the more you'll become like Him. His love will make you distinctly different.

Light for your path

Proverbs 10:12
John 15:9–12
Romans 8:38–39
1 Corinthians 13:4–8, 13
Ephesians 3:16–19
1 John 4:18

The day that each person willingly
accepts himself or herself for who
he or she is and acknowledges
the uniqueness of God's framing process
marks the beginning of a journey
to seeing the handiwork of God
in each life.

RAVI ZACHARIAS

Constructive Sorrow

*Because your heart was responsive and you
humbled yourself before the LORD…and
because you tore your robes
and wept in my presence, I also have
heard you, declares the LORD.*

2 KINGS 22:19 NIV

There is a time to be sorry. Likewise, there is an appropriate way to let your sorrow be known. No one gets through this life without needing to become humble and admit to wrongdoing once in a while. This is true in human relationships and in your relationship with God.

With God, you will find that honest confession concerning your missteps is one of the most positive and productive conversations you can have. God never holds grudges, and you will discover that the patience of God is without limits for those who earnestly seek to do His will. Not only is He patient, but He rushes to relieve the feelings of guilt that often weigh on your heart. Furthermore, His mercy is so lavish, He more than compensates for your sorrow, seeking to fill your heart with immediate peace, joy, and hope. In addition, the Spirit of God will give you counsel for the healing of human relationships where needed.

Seeking guidance from God's Word, consulting with friends who walk with God, and gleaning insight from spiritual counselors will provide invaluable wisdom concerning how to ask for forgiveness and work toward reconciliation with others. There is much to be gained through genuine sorrow.

Light for your path

Deuteronomy 11:26–28
Isaiah 48:17–18; 55:7
Matthew 9:13
Luke 6:46
Acts 26:20
Romans 2:4
2 Corinthians 7:9–10

God sees everything we've ever done
and He's willing to forgive.
But we must confess to Him.

RUTH BELL GRAHAM

An Unbreakable Commitment

The LORD watches the whole earth carefully and is ready to strengthen those who are devoted to him.

2 CHRONICLES 16:9 NET

When we commit ourselves to a relationship or job, we go into it with the intention of seeing it through. But for any number of reasons, we sometimes make the decision to break our commitment. Even spiritual commitments can fail. Sometimes we lose our resolve, or we find we have overcommitted ourselves, or we realize a particular spiritual practice is not drawing us closer to God. What then?

Unconditionally committed to you, your heavenly Father speaks no words of rejection. He has no wish to make you feel sad, but only to help you grow in spiritual wisdom. The words you will most often hear from Him are "try again." Try again with another book of devotions or a different Bible study group; change when or where you meditate and pray; adjust what you do with the time, energy, and resources God has made available to you today. Fulfill your commitment to Him by putting your trust in His unbreakable commitment to you.

Light for your path

Job 23:10
Psalm 40:1
Isaiah 40:31
Romans 5:3–5
Hebrews 10:36; 12:1
James 1:2–4
2 Peter 1:5–9

God will never, never, never let us down
if we have faith in Him.
He will always look after us.
So we must cleave to Jesus.
Our whole life must
simply be woven into Jesus.

MOTHER TERESA

Trust in the LORD with all your heart,
And lean not on your
own understanding;
In all your ways acknowledge Him,
And He shall direct your paths.

PROVERBS 3:5–6 NKJV

Helping Others Understand

*For Ezra had devoted himself
to the study and observance of the
Law of the LORD, and to teaching
its decrees and laws in Israel.*

EZRA 7:10 NIV

*I*t is one thing to gain understanding. It is quite another thing to live as if you have understanding. And it is something else altogether to help others understand.

Gaining insight into God—His ways and His will—may come through various means: study of His Word, listening to sermons, reading books on relevant topics, or even observing God's amazing creation. Your mind gets stretched out of its previous paradigm and expanded to receive the vast revelation of the incredible God that He is.

Taking the next step—putting your understanding into action—requires more than merely an intellectual exercise. Your heart and your will become engaged in the motivation and determination to conform your life to what you have learned. This moves you from the arena of knowledge into the realm of authentic experience, where character is forged, decisions are made, and people are deeply impacted. But even more—getting beyond yourself—you discover, at last, that helping someone else to know the Lord brings with it a joy and a measure of fulfillment unlike anything you've experienced yet. That joy multiplies—within the community of faith and within the heart of God.

Don't settle for mere understanding. Go beyond simply believing.

Light for your path

Deuteronomy 34:9
Ruth 1:16–18
2 Kings 2:1–15
Esther 2:10–11
Proverbs 17:17
2 Timothy 2:1–7
Hebrews 3:13

Our vertical growth in Christ cannot be disassociated from our horizontal growth with people around us.

JACK HAYFORD

12/19

Fragile Beauty

The joy of the LORD is your strength.
NEHEMIAH 8:10 KJV

Porcelain is known for its strength and translucence. Of course, *strength* is a relative term. While porcelain is strong for fired clay, it easily chips, cracks, and breaks. It will never win a battle against a slate floor. But this weakness doesn't make porcelain less attractive or desirable. In fact, its delicacy only adds to its beauty. Fine porcelain is so translucent that the shadow of the hand of the one holding it can typically be seen right through it.

The same can be said of you. It's true that God is a source of strength. But you're still fragile. Even your areas of greatest strength hold weaknesses and vulnerabilities. But God's Word tells you that He can use all of who you are, even your weaknesses, to do amazing things.

When you feel small or incapable of handling a task you know you have to face, pray for God's power to work mightily in your life. But remember to look for the shadow of His hand, gently holding you close. When you're weak, God's strength has a chance to shine through you in unexpectedly beautiful ways.

Light for your path

Psalm 27:1; 31:24; 105:4
Isaiah 40:28–31; 41:10
2 Corinthians 12:9–10
Ephesians 3:14–19; 6:10
Philippians 4:13

There are things that you
will only be able to learn
by the weakest among us.

GIANNA JESSEN

Coming alongside Others

Then they sat down with him on the ground for seven days and seven nights, yet no one spoke a word to him, for they saw that his pain was very great.

JOB 2:13 NET

How do we comfort those in trouble? First of all, it's hard to give what we haven't received. As we go through troubles of our own, we discover that, yes, good people have problems that sometimes don't go away. We discover that God always cares, always helps, always empowers us to move forward. None of us likes to have problems, but most of us can look back at our problems and see how God used them to make us into better, stronger people. Over the course of time, we learn what it is to be comforted and coached by God through our own troubles.

But none of that puts us in a position to completely understand why others are experiencing trouble or what that experience is like for them. We don't know how they feel, and often we will not have the answers for them—even when we think we do. What we can do, though, is offer the comfort we have received, the hope we have found, the presence of God that we have experienced in our times of struggle. When we invite God into the lives of those who are struggling, we give them a gift greater than any advice we could offer.

Light for your path

Isaiah 40:1; 66:13
John 11:35
1 Corinthians 14:3
2 Corinthians 1:3–4; 7:6
Galatians 6:2
1 Thessalonians 2:11–12

Our Lord does not care so much for
the importance of our works
as for the love
with which they are done.

SAINT TERESA OF AVILA

Hearing and Eye Exams

*My ears had heard of you
but now my eyes have seen you.*

JOB 42:5 NIV

For you to hear, your ears capture sound waves and translate these fluctuations into an electrical signal that your brain can understand. Your eyes are similarly complex and require a chemical reaction to convert light into electrical impulses that your brain reads as vision. Both your sense of hearing and your sense of sight rely on well-designed components working smoothly together.

In a spiritual sense, you were also intricately wired for keen hearing and sight. God formed you with an innate capacity for tuning in to His sounds and His sights. But sometimes you can depend a bit too much on the things people tell you about God instead of listening to Him yourself. You can also lean too strongly on what others tell you about seeing God work in their lives instead of looking for Him yourself.

To keep your hearing crisp for the resonance of God and your eyesight sharp for the landscapes of God in your life, why not sit still for a little checkup? Ask the Master Audiologist and Ophthalmologist to remove anything that is blocking you from hearing His specific message to you in His Word, and from seeing Him in your own day-to-day life. The good news is, He'll reveal Himself so that you can't miss Him.

Light for your path

Deuteronomy 4:29
1 Chronicles 16:11
Psalm 25:9, 12; 37:4, 7;
46:10; 73:24; 119:105
Acts 17:27

We must train ourselves in godliness
so we can quickly and decisively
recognize our Savior's voice.
When He speaks, we move.
When His Spirit nudges, we respond.

JONI EARECKSON TADA

In the Zone

LORD, who may abide in Your tabernacle?
Who may dwell in Your holy hill?
He who walks uprightly,
and works righteousness,
and speaks the truth in his heart.

PSALM 15:1–2 NKJV

You know you're "in the zone" when you're completely focused, your actions feel effortless, and everything clicks. It's like staying in the sweet spot when you golf, in peak performance as an athlete, or with optimal focus as a student. You need to find ways to stay balanced, because there's always something to pull you out of your zone. You must invest valuable time and energy in staying finely tuned to keep on task.

When you really feel like you're clicking with God, you are in your "God zone." There's life, peace, and joy in that zone. How do you keep that going? Obey God. Do what's right. Speak truthfully. "Obeying God" is God-language for "I love You, Lord, and I want to respect and model Your ways." Doing what is right is turning to His Word each day for direction and wise steps. Speaking truth is being loyal to God's integrity with your words because God is truth; He never lies. Ever. And a lie moves you away from His authentic presence.

Through obedience, doing what's right, and speaking truth, you can invest in your "God zone." It's worth it.

Light for your path

Deuteronomy 11:26–28
1 Samuel 15:22
Isaiah 48:17–18
Luke 6:46
John 14:15, 21
1 Peter 2:13–16
1 John 2:5

Let us never suppose that obedience
is impossible or that holiness
is meant only for a select few.
Our Shepherd leads us
in paths of righteousness—
not for our name's sake, but for His.

ELISABETH ELLIOT

Making Our Way Clear

*The steps of a good man are ordered by
the LORD, and He delights in his way.*

PSALM 37:23 NKJV

Have you ever watched ants? Ants often have an interesting way of walking. They take a few steps, and then they stop. They take a few more steps, and then they stop.

The Christian life functions in much the same way. We take a few steps, and then we stop to get more direction for our journey. Then we correct our course if we need to, and take a few more steps. It's much like driving through the fog. When we drive through the fog, we don't take anything for granted. We don't know what the next two hundred yards of the road will bring. So we slow down and drive according to the visibility ahead.

This step-by-step, day-by-day process is how God works. He could, of course, give us our entire life plan, complete with contingencies, early on. But He doesn't. He clears enough fog out of the way so that we can find our way forward a little bit. Then we look back to Him. Our time alone with God affords us the opportunity to clear the fog, to get the course corrections we need, and to get back on track and stay on track. Looking to God makes our way clear.

Light for your path

Deuteronomy 29:29
Psalm 18:30; 25:4–5
Proverbs 3:5–6
Isaiah 2:3; 41:10; 55:8–9
Jeremiah 32:40
Micah 6:8
Romans 8:28; 11:33–36
1 Corinthians 2:9–10, 16
James 1:5–6

We walk without fear, full of hope
and courage and strength to do His will,
waiting for the endless good
which He is always giving as fast
as He can get us able to take it in.

GEORGE MACDONALD

God speaks to us from His Word,
the Bible. It...supplies His voice
in every area of our lives.
It is the road map for your success
at school, work, in your marriage,
with your friends, everything!

Ron Channell

Spiritual Satisfaction

O God, You are my God; I shall seek You earnestly; my soul thirsts for You, my flesh yearns for You, in a dry and weary land.

PSALM 63:1 NASB

Spiritual hunger is deeper than physical hunger. The growl of emptiness in our souls is a feeling more than a sound. Its rumblings are dissatisfaction with life, yearning for something more, questioning God's goodness and fairness. Like a physical appetite, the pangs start small and grow to screaming proportions. You know the feeling if you've ever felt empty after reaching a long-sought-after goal. You know the feeling if life feels flat even though you are doing all the things you thought would make you happy. You just want more. That inner emptiness is your yellow warning light, cautioning you to turn around and get some food fast, but not fast food.

Fast foods for the soul are the morsels that fill your eyes—TV, romance novels, adventure movies—but leave your spirit empty. The quest ends as you turn your search to God. Spiritual hunger can only be satisfied by time spent alone with God, opening your Bible to learn about Jesus and doing what He says will fill you up. Praise and worship are like a feast. God alone satisfies the hunger of your soul.

Light for your path

Psalm 37:4; 90:14; 107:8–9; 119:35
Isaiah 55:2
Matthew 5:6
John 4:13–14; 6:35
Philippians 4:11–13

Because the face of God is so lovely,
my brothers and sisters, so beautiful,
once you have seen it,
nothing else can give you pleasure.
It will give insatiable satisfaction
of which we will never tire.
We shall always be hungry
and always have our fill.

AUGUSTINE

Embracing Simplicity

Oh, satisfy us early with Your mercy,
that we may rejoice
and be glad all our days!

PSALM 90:14 NKJV

*E*mbracing simplicity" doesn't mean living on a subsistence level. It does mean seeing the material trappings of life as mere adornments—and finding true peace and fulfillment in your relationship with God and in those qualities that He has placed within you.

Most of us realize that mere survival is not what God intended for His people. However, the abundance we enjoy on the outside can blind us to the spiritual abundance God has provided for us. What does that mean? It means that God offers each of us the gifts and grace we need to make the most of the life we've been given and to help others do the same without having to rely on material possessions for contentment.

The place to begin is in your personal time alone with God. It is there, in His presence, that you will see the bigger picture. When viewed from the perspective of eternity, many of the concerns of this material world will diminish in importance. Ask God to give you the grace to live in anticipation of the joys that are to come. When you do, you will find life to be so much simpler.

Light for your path

Job 1:21
Psalm 23:1–2; 37:4; 46:10
Philippians 4:4–6, 11–12
1 Timothy 6:6–8
Hebrews 13:5
2 Peter 1:3

Blessed are the single-hearted,
for they shall enjoy much peace.
If you refuse to be hurried and pressed,
if you stay your soul on God,
nothing can keep you from that clearness
of spirit which is life and peace.
In that stillness you will know
what His will is.

AMY CARMICHAEL

Gratitude, the Ideal Gift

Give thanks to the LORD, for he is good;
his love endures forever.

PSALM 107:1 NIV

Want to know a great gift idea for God? It's gratitude. You don't have to wait for a special occasion. Gratitude is a gift you can give every day of the year. The funny thing is, the more you give, the more you'll discover you have on hand. Cultivating a grateful heart begins by slowing down long enough to notice what you have. Consider it anti-advertising. The goal of any advertising campaign is to direct people's attention toward what they're missing, to leave them feeling discontent with what they've been given.

Gratitude reminds you of what you already have, of gifts easily taken for granted. These can be as small as the beauty of an almond tree in bloom or as large as the gift of your very next breath. When you recognize that every good gift ultimately comes from God, you can't help but feel grateful. This deepens the pleasure of even an ordinary day, making you not only more content, but more generous with what you've received. Gratitude is a gift that simply can't stop giving.

Light for your path

Psalm 92:1; 100:1–5; 103:1–5
Ephesians 1:16; 5:20
Colossians 3:15–17
1 Thessalonians 5:18
Hebrews 12:28; 13:15
James 1:17

*God has two dwellings:
one in heaven, and the other
in a meek and thankful heart.*

Izaak Walton

*When you experience grace and are loved when
you do not deserve it, you spend the rest of your life
standing on tiptoes trying to reach His plan
for your life out of gratitude.*

Charles Stanley

God's Flashlight

*Your word is a lamp to my feet
and a light to my path.*

PSALM 119:105 NKJV

Children are often afraid of the dark. They think that if there isn't any light in a room, it isn't safe to go in. As adults, we are not as often afraid of the dark, of course, but we're not crazy about it, either.

Walking in the dark can be dangerous. Walking off the path God wants us to follow is dangerous too. But the Bible shows us the right path and helps us stay on it. It's kind of like having a flashlight at night. It helps you feel safe and keeps you out of trouble.

Think of a time when you were struggling. Think about why darkness can be so scary. Go into a dark room or out into the dark night and just stand there for a few moments. Then turn on a flashlight. Makes quite a difference in how you see things and feel about the situation, right? The Bible can bring that same kind of illumination to your life. God lights the path when you trust in Him.

Light for your path

Exodus 13:21; 14:20
2 Samuel 23:3–4
Nehemiah 9:19
Job 33:28
Psalm 18:28; 36:9; 43:3; 44:3;
118:27; 119:105–112, 130
Isaiah 9:2; 60:1, 19
Micah 7:8
Matthew 5:14
John 1:4–5, 7–9; 8:12

*His life is our light—our purpose
and meaning and reason for living.*

ANNE GRAHAM LOTZ

*God's guidance is even more important
than common sense.
I can declare that the deepest darkness
is outshone by the light of Jesus.*

CORRIE TEN BOOM

Picture Perfect

*How good and how pleasant it is
for brothers to dwell together in unity!*

PSALM 133:1 NASB

A puzzle is a great example of unity. Each distinctive piece interlocks with those around it. Together, they form a picture that can only be seen when every piece is in its proper place. God calls His children to be "one" in Him. But unity doesn't equal uniformity. At times, this causes division. One woman raises her hands while singing in church. Another doesn't feel comfortable being that demonstrative.

God's children worship, pray, celebrate communion, and interpret the Bible in different ways. After all, God designed us to be individuals. It's healthy to discuss our differences. But after all is said and done, we need to pull together as one. Together, God's children create a picture of what God's like. We're on display for the world to see. The more closely we're unified in love, the more accurate that picture will be.

Light for your path

John 17:23
Romans 6:5
1 Corinthians 1:10; 12:12–26
Ephesians 4:1–6, 11–13
Philippians 2:1–3
Colossians 3:14

To gather with God's people in united adoration of the Father is as necessary to the Christian life as prayer.

MARTIN LUTHER

The invisible bond that unites all believers to Christ is far more tender, and lasting, and precious; and, as we come to recognize and realize that we are all dwelling in one sphere of life in Him, we learn to look on every believer as our brother, in a sense that is infinitely higher than all human relationships.

A. T. PIERSON

Three Little Words

*The LORD's delight is in those who
fear him, those who put their hope
in his unfailing love.*

PSALM 147:11 NLT

They're on billboards, bumper stickers, T-shirts, even toothbrushes. Three little words so central in His Word: *God loves you.* This statement is tossed about so casually these days, it's almost cliché. But don't let familiarity with the phrase diminish the power of the truth behind it. It's not a feel-good motto. It's a steadfast promise. It's the assurance that God (the Almighty Creator and Ruler of everything) loves (sacrificially, unconditionally, and eternally cares for and is devoted to) you. It's true that God loves everyone in the world. But He doesn't love you just because you're a part of that mass of humanity. He loves you as an individual. And the good news doesn't stop there.

The Bible says that not only does God love you, but He delights in you. When you *delight* in something, you *celebrate* it. You take joy in every detail. Picture a new mother so delighted with her child that she can't help but smile every time she catches sight of her child's face. You are that child. Take time to delight in your Father's love for you today.

Light for your path

Jeremiah 31:3
John 3:16; 13:34–35; 15:13–16
Romans 5:8; 8:38–39
1 Corinthians 13:1–13
Ephesians 2:4–7
1 John 3:1; 4:7–18

The grace of God means something like:
Here is your life. You might never have
been, but you are because the party
wouldn't have been complete without you.
Here is the world. Beautiful and terrible
things will happen. Don't be afraid.
I am with you. Nothing can ever
separate us. It's for you I created
the universe. I love you.

FREDERICK BUECHNER

Never doubt in the dark
what God has shown you
in the light.

EDITH EDMAN

Luster of Love

As in water the face is reflected as a face, so a person's heart reflects the person.

PROVERBS 27:19 NET

If you wear silver jewelry, you probably have noticed that it tends to tarnish. When that happens, a little rubbing with a treated cloth returns the item back to its original luster. When God created you, He intended for you to reflect His glorious image. Talk about luster! But chances are, you may feel intimidated by God's high expectations. That's why He rushes to assure you that He has taken on the responsibility of restoring your original shine.

As you continue to read about Him, pray to Him, and think about Him during your day, He is doing the work of making you more reflective of His glory. Through the gift of His Spirit in you, God turns your heart toward His will and sets your eyes on His ways. More and more, the shine of joy and contentment brightens your life, and the sheen of gentleness and peace touches those around you.

As you can see your face reflected in a perfectly polished piece of silver, others can see God's face reflected in the luster of your God-given love.

Light for your path

Psalm 23:3; 51:12; 145:14
Isaiah 53:1–5
Jeremiah 30:17
Joel 2:25
Matthew 12:13
2 Corinthians 5:17

Transformation comes, in the end,
not from an act of will, but an act of grace.
We can only ask for it and keep asking.

PHILIP YANCEY

*Live your lives in love, the same sort of love
which Christ gives us, and which He perfectly expressed
when He gave Himself as a sacrifice to God.*

CORRIE TEN BOOM

The Presence of Love

I am my beloved's, and my beloved is mine. He feeds his flock among the lilies.

SONG OF SOLOMON 6:3 NKJV

When you're in love with someone, a walk in the rain becomes a welcome chance to share an umbrella. An unexpected snowstorm provides the setting for a quiet afternoon snuggled in front of the fireplace together. What could be bad times are good when you are with the one you love.

In the same way, a growing love for God and appreciation for His presence beside you can give you a whole new outlook on life's storms. From a short-lived cloudburst to a long and difficult winter, adversity offers yet another occasion to draw closer to the Lord you love—and who loves you even more. His Word is very clear about that. Nothing can happen to you that would be too small for His protective hand.

Nothing you will ever face could be too serious, too difficult, or too long lasting to keep the warmth and closeness of His comfort away from your heart either. When you're in love with someone, suddenly nothing matters quite so much as the fact that you are with your beloved and your beloved is with you.

Light for your path

Deuteronomy 10:12
Matthew 22:37–40
John 13:34–35; 14:21–24
Romans 12:9–10
1 John 3:14; 4:7–21

Christ is with us,
and the warmth is contagious.

JONI EARECKSON TADA

Love is there for us, love so great that it does not
turn its face away from us. That Love is Jesus.
We can dare to hope and believe again.

GLORIA GAITHER

God's Megaphone

*The people walking in darkness
have seen a great light.*
ISAIAH 9:2 NIV

Prophets were people chosen by God to speak for Him. And Isaiah was a super-mega prophet—one of the greatest prophets ever. If they had dictionaries in Jerusalem in 700 B.C. and you had looked up the word *prophet*, it would talk about Isaiah! Isaiah was God's megaphone to the people of Judah (remember, the country had split in two: Israel became the northern part, and Judah the southern part).

And while Isaiah did a lot of preaching about turning away from sin, he also made some major prophetic predictions—including truths about Jesus Christ! Even the structure of the book is prophetic in some ways: It has sixty-six chapters, just like the Bible has sixty-six books. The first section of thirty-nine chapters starts with Israel's sin. The first thirty-nine books of the Bible (the Old Testament) begin with Adam and Eve's sin and catalogs the many sins of Israel. The last twenty-seven chapters of Isaiah are about God offering forgiveness and hope to everyone, just like the last twenty-seven books of the Bible (the New Testament) offer Jesus Christ, our only Source of forgiveness and hope, to the whole world.

Isaiah wrote this hundreds of years before the New Testament books were even written. That is a megaphone for eternity.

Light for your path

Isaiah 7:14; 9:2–7; 11:1–2, 4–5, 10;
40:3–8; 42:6–9; 53:1–8, 12; 61:1–2
Matthew 2:1–6
Luke 2:4–5, 7–15
John 8:31–32; 14:16
1 Peter 2:24
1 John 1:1–3
Revelation 1:5–6

At the very heart and foundation
of all God's dealings with us, however...
mysterious they may be, we must dare
to believe in and assert the infinite,
unmerited, and unchanging love of God.

L. B. Cowman

12/23

God's Place of Peace

*You will keep in perfect peace
all who trust in you, all whose
thoughts are fixed on you!*

Isaiah 26:3 NLT

Today's headlines suggest that peace is not just improbable, but impossible. Wars, earthquakes, injustice, global warming, economic instability—world events proclaim that we live in a time of chaos, when life is destined to go from bad to worse. But our heavenly Father is a God of order, not chaos. Even in the direst of circumstances, He reaches out to us and offers us a place of peace. The world around us may feel as though it's falling apart, but inside, God's putting us together "piece by peace."

Take your eyes off the brokenness around you. Focus on God and His promises. Allow His Spirit to bathe your heart and mind in the reality of God's big picture, His eternal purpose and plan.

Trust that God has both the power and the desire to bring something good out of every situation. Breathe deep, every breath a prayer. Peace is more than a Christmas wish or the hope of potential beauty queens. It's God's gift to you today. Receive it with open arms.

Light for your path

Psalm 34:14; 119:165
Isaiah 26:3; 48:18
John 14:27; 16:33
Romans 5:1; 8:6; 14:17–19
Philippians 4:6–7
Colossians 3:15

*Prayer guards hearts
and minds and causes God
to bring peace out of chaos.*

Beth Moore

*All God's glory and beauty come from within,
and there He delights to dwell.
His visits there are frequent,
His conversation sweet,
His comforts refreshing,
His peace passing all understanding.*

Thomas à Kempis

Letting God Lead

*The LORD said to His people:
"You are standing at the crossroads.
So consider your path. Ask where the old,
reliable paths are. Ask where the path
is that leads to blessing and follow it.
If you do, you will find rest for your souls."*
JEREMIAH 6:16 NET

Looking to an invisible God for guidance is a bit like learning to make your way through the world while wearing a blindfold. You become more attuned to the little things: the slope of the sidewalk leading down to a pedestrian crossing, the subtle difference in the sound of your footsteps as you draw closer to a wall, the smell of the bakery letting you know you're only a block from home. The more you walk the same path, the more familiar it becomes. In time, you realize you can walk confidently by faith, instead of by sight.

When you're uncertain which way to turn, turn first to God. You'll discover you already have some of the information you need. Is your decision supported by what you read in the Bible? Have others who follow God counseled you to head this way? Has God's Spirit given you peace about moving forward? If so, take the first step. Keep leaning on God as you move ahead. He'll lead you where you need to go.

Light for your path

Psalm 37:23; 143:10
Proverbs 2:3–5; 3:5–6
Micah 6:8
Romans 12:2
Ephesians 5:17–18
James 1:5

God has His reasons.
He has His purposes.
Ours is an intentional God,
brimming over with motive and mission.
He never does things capriciously
or decides with the flip of a coin.

JONI EARECKSON TADA

The Meaning of Your Life

"For I know what I have planned for you," says the LORD. "I have plans to prosper you, not to harm you. I have plans to give you a future filled with hope."

JEREMIAH 29:11 NET

What's the meaning of life? That question will never go away, no matter how many answers are given. How do you answer that question? As important as it is, you have an even more critical question to answer: What's the meaning of *your* life?

Though you may not realize it, God has infused your life with purpose and meaning. Reflect on that thought and its ramifications. What if your life has a purpose beyond what you can see? Even if your life's work is already filled with purpose—if you spend the day training young minds to acquire knowledge and learn to navigate the adult world, or if you help save the lives of critically wounded people who are rushed to the emergency room—consider the possibility that God wants even *more* for your life. Not *from* you, but *for* you.

Take that possibility to God in prayer. Ask Him what more He has for you. Maybe it's imparting His wisdom to the next generation, or restoring souls, not just bodies, to a healthy condition. Listen for the answers He gives you. When you discover the meaning of your life, the answer to the larger question tends to fall in place.

Light for your path

Joshua 1:7

Proverbs 4:25–27; 14:15; 16:9

Jeremiah 10:23

John 15:16

Acts 26:16

Ephesians 4:1–3

Philippians 3:13–14

Faith is not belief without proof,

but trust without reservations.

ELTON TRUEBLOOD

God prepared a plan for your life alone—
and neither man nor the devil can destroy that plan.

KAY ARTHUR

Call to me and I will answer you.

I'll tell you marvelous
and wondrous things
that you could never
figure out on your own.

JEREMIAH 33:3 MSG

Our Provider

*They will be radiant with joy over the
good things the LORD provides.*

JEREMIAH 31:12 NET

When the Israelites were in the wilderness, God provided manna—a strange but wonderful, ready-to-eat food—in a culture where preparing a meal usually involved slaughtering an animal. This stuff appeared daily on the ground, ready for consumption. In instructing them to collect enough for only one day, God was trying to train them to trust Him. Day after day after day, they had what they needed, and they could see that God could be trusted. But once they ate the produce of the promised land much later in their journey, the manna was no longer waiting for them in the morning (Joshua 5:12).

Given God's track record of provision in the wilderness and His unmistakable instructions to take only what was needed daily, it makes sense to trust Him with our needs and the needs of our family. Do we have enough trust in Him today to walk away from a sure thing, or would we open wide our hands and sweep as much onto our plates as we could?

Decide today to believe what His Word says: He rewards those who diligently seek Him. Where there are questions about how things have turned out in the past, remember His faithfulness in the midst of it, and trust Him even with the questions unanswered.

Light for your path

Nehemiah 9:15, 20, 27
Psalm 23:1; 81:10; 105:39–40;
132:12–18
Luke 12:22–24
Philippians 4:19–20

The act of thanksgiving
is a demonstration of the fact
that you are going to trust
and believe God.

KAY ARTHUR

*We can be certain that God will give us the strength
and resources we need to live through any situation in life
that he ordains. The will of God will never take us
where the grace of God cannot sustain us.*

BILLY GRAHAM

Overcoming Anxiety

*Do not lose heart or be afraid
when rumors are heard in the land;
one rumor comes this year, another
the next, rumors of violence in
the land and of ruler against ruler.*

JEREMIAH 51:46 NIV

What makes you anxious or causes you to worry? Every person has her own unique list. Snakes and big hairy bugs may be on yours. But it's just as likely to include things like air travel, water, heights, enclosed spaces, or public speaking. Then there are the more personal fears: "Will my mammogram be okay?" "Will I lose my job?" "Will my husband leave me?" Anxiety can stop even a bold, confident woman in her tracks.

When you come face-to-face with something you fear, remember that you never face your fears alone. God is with you. Like a valiant warrior, He fights for and protects you. He wants to replace your fears with His peace. When your heart begins to race, turn to God. Ask Him to help you sift what's rational from what's irrational. If there's a real need for caution, He can provide the wisdom you need to know what you should do. Finally, take courage. Knowing that God is near can give you the strength you need to face whatever comes your way.

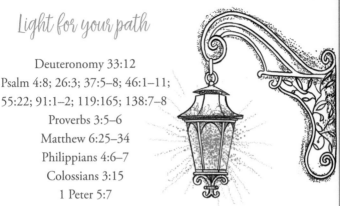

Light for your path

Deuteronomy 33:12
Psalm 4:8; 26:3; 37:5–8; 46:1–11;
55:22; 91:1–2; 119:165; 138:7–8
Proverbs 3:5–6
Matthew 6:25–34
Philippians 4:6–7
Colossians 3:15
1 Peter 5:7

Counting His graces has awakened me
to how He cherishes me, holds me,
passionately values me.... I can trust.

ANN VOSKAMP

Fear and doubt are conquered by a faith that rejoices.
And faith can rejoice because the promises
of God are as certain as God Himself.

KAY ARTHUR

12/28

Our Return

*"Then you shall know that
I am the LORD, that you may remember
and be ashamed, and never open your
mouth anymore...when I provide you
an atonement for all you have done,"
says the Lord GOD.*

EZEKIEL 16:62–63 NKJV

One of the most famous stories in the Bible is the parable of the prodigal son. Jesus shares how a young man took his family inheritance, went off on his own, squandered his wealth with reckless living, and ended up in utter poverty. Realizing that the pigs he was feeding for a living had it better than he did, he decided to go back home. But he couldn't go back as a son because he has disgraced the family name. Perhaps, however, his father will allow him to be a servant. Not sure of the outcome, the young man started for home. On the way, he rehearsed the speech in his mind. *I'm not worthy to be your son,* he says over and over again. But from a long way off, his father saw him and came running to meet him. "I'm not worthy to be your son," he began. But the father wasn't listening. His son had returned!

The parable, of course, is an illustration of our relationship with God. The moment we turn back to Him and humble ourselves in His presence, He stops listening to our faults and sets the table for a celebration.

Light for your path

Psalm 139:1–18
Proverbs 28:13
Isaiah 55:7
Lamentations 3:22–23
Luke 15:11–24
Revelation 2:4–5

I have sought Your nearness;
With all my heart have I called You,
and going out to meet You
I found You coming toward me.

YEHUDA HALEVI

The Indwelling Spirit

*I will put my Spirit in you
and move you to follow my decrees
and be careful to keep my laws.*

EZEKIEL 36:27 NIV

What's the easiest way to take the air out of a drinking glass? Simple. Fill it with water. If we tried to remove the air without first putting something in its place, what would happen? The glass would shatter, not strong enough to hold an airless vacuum.

Spiritually speaking, we are the same way. By ourselves, we are empty containers. We are designed to be filled with something. Apart from God, we humans turn to all sorts of things to fill up the emptiness inside. But none of those things fully satisfy.

God understands this. That's why He invites you to be filled with His Spirit. God, in the person of His Holy Spirit, wants to live inside you. He wants to fill every "room" in your "house." He wants to be your comfort. When He enters painful places in your heart, you find peace. When He enters confused places in your heart, you find clarity. When He enters grieving places, you find joy. When He enters your frustrating experiences, you discover a patience that takes hard things and makes them easy. When He enters your relationships, you experience love. As you invite the Holy Spirit in, you become whole.

Light for your path

John 14:16–17, 26
Acts 1:8
Romans 5:5; 8:9, 11
1 Corinthians 2:16; 6:19; 12:11
Ephesians 1:13–14; 5:18
Hebrews 9:14

The amount of power you experience to live a victorious, triumphant Christian life is directly proportional to the freedom you give the Spirit to be Lord of your life!

ANNE GRAHAM LOTZ

In the Storm

But Jonah had gone down
into the lowest parts of the ship,
had lain down, and was fast asleep.

JONAH 1:5 NKJV

The Bible tells us the stories of two men who slept on a boat during a storm. The first man was Jonah, a prophet. God wanted him to walk into the capital city of an enemy nation and warn them of impending judgment. Jonah couldn't bring himself to do it, so he ran away from God. He took passage on a ship headed in the opposite direction, and as it set sail, he went below deck and fell into a deep sleep. While he slept, a terrible storm tossed the ship.

The other sleeper was Jesus (Mark 4:35–41). It was time to cross the lake. A group of experienced fishermen were at the helm. Jesus fell asleep. After He did, a furious storm threatened to swamp the boat.

Both men were sleeping. Both needed to be awakened. But there the similarity ends. Jonah was sleeping the sleep of escape. He was trying to push God out of his life. Jesus was sleeping within the embrace of His Father.

Storms enter our lives. If we are running from God, like Jonah, a storm can stop us dead in our tracks. But if we linger in God's presence, like Jesus, a storm merely reveals our great calm within.

Light for your path

Psalm 32:6–7; 37:24, 39; 46:1–3
Matthew 6:25–34
John 14:27
Romans 8:28
2 Corinthians 1:3–4
1 Peter 1:7

*If God has you in the palm
of His hand and your real life
is secure in Him, then you can
venture forth—into the places
and relationships, the challenges,
the very heart of the storm—
and you will be safe there.*

PAULA RINEHART

Praying for Understanding

*Do not be afraid, Daniel, for from the first day
that you set your heart on understanding
this and on humbling yourself before
your God, your words were heard,
and I have come in response to your words.*

DANIEL 10:12 NASB

Once we've developed the habit of daily time with God, we find ourselves longing more and more for the hour to roll around again. The delight we experience in intimacy with the Lord compels us to seek Him with more and more passion and frequency. And we delight to discover that He is as anxious to be with us as we are to be with Him.

One of the most thrilling discoveries comes with having asked the Lord for understanding and then receiving the insight for which we asked. The first time it occurs, it staggers us somewhat. We are tempted to question whether it might just be coincidence. It happens again, causing us to suspect that something intentional is going on. It happens a third time, and we begin to catch on to the faithfulness of God in response to those who seek Him.

The Scriptures indicate that the very moment you register an inquiry before the Lord, His response is dispatched in the heavens. Depending upon the situation, it could take weeks or even years before the answer is perceptible to you, or it could be instantaneous, even as you ask. The important thing is, you can relax. His answer is on its way.

Light for your path

Matthew 6:6–7
Mark 11:24
John 14:13–14; 15:7
Ephesians 3:12; 6:18
Philippians 4:6
1 Timothy 2:8
Hebrews 4:16
James 5:16

Prayer is not overcoming
God's reluctance.
It is laying hold of His willingness.

JULIAN OF NORWICH

I believe the Bible is the best gift
God has ever given to us.
All the good from
the Savior of the world

is communicated to us
through this book.

ABRAHAM LINCOLN

Forgiving Ourselves

Where is another God like you,
who pardons the guilt of the remnant,
overlooking the sins of his special people?

MICAH 7:18 NLT

Sometimes it is easier to forgive others than it is to forgive ourselves. Some of us are so conscientious that the slightest slip-up leaves us wallowing in self-condemnation. Some of us feel that we've committed a sin so horrible that even God could not forgive us. Some of us know in our heads that God has forgiven us, but we don't feel it in our hearts. If this is a struggle for you, here are some questions for you to process in the Lord's presence the next time you are alone with Him: If those feelings of guilt and shame could talk, what would they say? What would happen if you stopped punishing yourself? How did these messages become part of your life? There are no right or wrong answers here, just honest and dishonest ones. The more honest we can be with the Lord, the more He is in a position to transform us.

Don't forget to ask Him for the truth about all of this. Who are you really? Jesus needs to answer that for you. Once He does, you will never be the same again. Forgiving yourself is not only possible, it's easy once you discover what God says about you.

Light for your path

Psalm 32:1–7; 51:1–19; 103:12
Isaiah 43:18
Matthew 5:44; 6:14–15; 18:21–22
Mark 11:25
Luke 11:4; 17:3; 23:34
Romans 15:5–7
Ephesians 4:31–32
Colossians 3:13
1 Peter 2:23; 3:9
1 John 1:9

God is offering Himself to you daily,
and the rate of exchange is fixed:
your sins for His forgiveness,
your hurt for His balm of healing,
your sorrow for His joy.

BARBARA JOHNSON

Why Worry?

So then, do not worry about tomorrow,
for tomorrow will worry about itself.
Today has enough trouble of its own.

MATTHEW 6:34 NET

Picture your mind as a pot of cool, still water sitting on the stove. Then picture worry powering the heating element beneath it. A little fretting here and there sets the water simmering, disturbing the once-smooth surface as bubbles begin to roil. Now, turn up the heat a bit more. Mild concern becomes anxiety. Before long, this boils over into full-fledged panic.

Where's God when you need to turn down the heat? As always, God is here. He's already given you all you need to keep worry in the OFF position. When you find yourself concerned about something, refuse to let things heat up. Point your concern upward instead of inward. Dwelling on the "what ifs" of life has the power to do nothing but give off steam.

Releasing every care into God's hands is like letting a bubble take flight. Before you know it, it's no longer in sight. Refuse to let worries disturb your peace of mind. Let God take the heat.

Light for your path

Deuteronomy 33:12
Psalm 4:8; 26:3; 37:5–8; 46:1–11;
55:22; 91:1–2; 119:65; 138:7–8
Proverbs 3:5–6
Matthew 6:25–34
Philippians 4:6–7
Colossians 3:15
1 Peter 5:7

*Worries carry responsibilities
that belong to God, not to you.
Worry does not enable us to escape evil;
it makes us unfit to cope with it
when it comes.*

CORRIE TEN BOOM

*And as we let our light shine, we unconsciously
give other people permission to do the same.
As we are liberated from our own fear,
our presence automatically liberates others.*

NELSON MANDELA

God's Plan

What do you want me to do for you?

MATTHEW 20:32 NIV

How do you discover God's plan for your life? How do you find God's plan for today? Is it really a matter of sacrificing all your own plans, giving up your own desires, canceling your own identity? Usually not. Yes, it is true that we submit to God. It is true that when God's desires and our desires conflict, we must yield to Him, knowing that He is wiser than we are. But as a rule, God works through our desires to move us in the direction of the plan He has for us.

God is a dance partner, not a puppet master. Your dreams matter to God. You bring your questions to Him: "Whom should I marry?" "Where should I live?" "What job should I choose?" "How should I spend the weekend?" "What should I buy?" But, in return, He asks: "What do you want?" That becomes the starting point for a conversation with God that may include counsel from others, searching the Bible, and the quiet voice of God's Spirit within you.

What do you want? In your time alone with Him, this is one of the things that He wants you to share with Him.

Light for your path

Joshua 1:8
Psalm 23:1–3; 31:3; 32:8;
37:23; 48:14; 119:105
Proverbs 3:5–6; 16:3, 9
Isaiah 30:21; 48:17
John 16:13
James 1:5

God wants to invade your life
and do great things. Will you take
that next step towards a deeper
relationship with God? God is saying,
"Trust Me, I won't let you fail.
I am for you not against you.
I want you to succeed. Just trust Me."

RYAN HAWLEY

Fear Not

Be of good cheer!
It is I; do not be afraid.

MARK 6:50 NKJV

Fear can claw at our minds and hearts and squeeze the joy out of life. If we stop to think about it, most of us fear dozens of things every single day. We fear being late for work, we fear being involved in a car accident, we fear the disapproval of others. Some of us dread dental appointments, financial slowdowns, and aging. Fear is cloaked in big and small packages that unexpectedly and frequently arrive on our doorstep.

Yet our fear, worry, and apprehension are no surprise to God. Although He doesn't experience trepidation at anything, He understands us when we balk at challenges or panic when we are pained. Countless times throughout His Word, God confidently reassures us that we can gain courage and "fear not." Yet He doesn't just command our bravery; He nudges us to let go of our anxiety and apprehensions by shifting our thinking.

How do we practically deal with those never-ending fears? By remembering throughout the day that we are not alone, because God—who is infinitely greater than any intimidating person or any daunting situation—is right beside us. When reminded of God's promises in His Word that He will never leave us nor forsake us, we can be sure that He is constantly on our side. We can stand up to our fears and watch our worry take a run for the hills.

Light for your path

Exodus 14:14
Deuteronomy 7:21
Joshua 1:5–9
Psalm 18:29–33; 27:14; 31:24
Isaiah 40:29–31; 41:10; 43:2–3; 50:7
Acts 4:13–31
Ephesians 6:10–18

*I discovered that sorrow was not
to be feared but rather endured
with hope and expectancy that God
would use it to visit and bless my life.*

JILL BRISCOE

Be Careful, Little Eyes

Your eye is the lamp of your body.

I haven't always filled my mind with the greatest things. Sometimes I watch movies or TV shows I probably shouldn't. And there's so much more junk out there in magazines, on the Internet, and in music that just isn't good for people who want to grow closer to God.

I need to be more careful about what I see and hear. Every day I have to make decisions about the kind of stuff I let into my life. And this passage reminds me to make choices that fill me with light, not darkness. Jesus is a shining light, and His love allows me to shine too. I don't want to let the darkness of the world block out God's light in me. What are you reading, watching, or listening to that is blocking God's light? Or what is blocking your light from shining on your friends and family? If you don't know, ask God to reveal to you any areas of darkness in your life.

The eyes are the portal through which God's light comes in and your light shines out. The children's song has it right, "Oh, be careful, little eyes, what you see!"

Light for your path

Psalm 18:28
Isaiah 9:2
Matthew 5:13–16
Luke 11:33–36
John 8:12
Acts 13:47

Faith is the strength by which
a shattered world shall emerge
into the light.

HELEN KELLER

*We are told to let our light shine, and if it does,
we won't need to tell anybody it does.
Lighthouses don't fire cannons to call attention
to their shining—they just shine.*

D. L. MOODY

The Little Things

The one who is faithful in a very little is also faithful in much.

Some say it's the little things in life that matter most: the way you let another driver merge in front of you, the words of appreciation you share with someone, the sips of pretend tea from a child's plastic tea set. Little things on earth magnify into big things in heaven.

God doesn't miss the minute gestures you do for others, which actually you are doing for Him. The beloved Mother Teresa often spoke of doing a small bit for others as a reflection of serving Jesus. A smile. A hug. A shared tear. All these seemingly modest and minor actions carry eternal significance.

This is why when you reserve time to sit alone with God and read your Bible, it matters. When you talk to Him throughout your busy days and thank Him "just because," it matters. Every time you turn your thoughts toward inviting God into your minutes and hours, it matters. In a world obsessed with gaining attention and admiring more visible possessions and more vocal people, it is wise at times to pursue the opposite. Instead of bigger, stronger, faster, higher, why not aspire to the little, often unseen, gestures of love? Even if others do not notice, God certainly will.

Light for your path

Micah 6:8
1 Corinthians 15:58
Galatians 6:9
Philippians 1:27
2 Thessalonians 3:13
Hebrews 3:6–8; 12:1
1 Peter 5:8

Be faithful in small things
because it is in them
that your strength lies.

MOTHER TERESA

The million little things that drop into your hands,
the small opportunities each day brings,
He leaves us free to use or abuse,
and goes unchanging along His silent way.

HELEN KELLER

I would rather
walk with God in the dark
than go alone in the light.

MARY GARDINER BRAINARD

Jesus, Your Friend

No longer do I call you servants,
for a servant does not know
what his master is doing;
but I have called you friends.

John 15:15 nkjv

*I*n a culture in which the word *friend* can be used as a verb and defined to include the complete strangers who follow you on Facebook, it's no wonder that the concept of friendship has been diluted. But when tragedy, grief, or adverse circumstances strike your life, you know full well who will be there to offer a comforting hug and a helping hand. It will be the flesh-and-blood people who enhance the quality of your life through their genuine friendship.

In one of the many great paradoxes of your life with God, the closest friend you have isn't one of those flesh-and-blood people, nor is it one of your online buddies. It's Jesus Himself. He's the most faithful and trustworthy friend you'll ever have, and what's more, He's always with you. He will never leave you. No matter how impressive it may seem to have thousands of online friends, having Jesus as your friend is one fact of your life that can be accurately described as awesome. As with any friendship, your relationship with Jesus depends in part on commitment and communication. By spending time with Him and engaging in conversation with Him, listening to Him as well as talking to Him, you show Jesus your dedication to your friendship with Him.

Light for your path

1 Samuel 18:1–3
Proverbs 13:20; 17:9, 17;
18:24; 22:24–25
Ecclesiastes 4:9–10
Matthew 18:20
John 13:14–15; 15:12–15
Acts 2:42–47
Philippians 2:3–4
1 Peter 4:8

The capacity to discern and do
the will of God arises out of friendship
with God, cultivated through prayer,
times of quiet listening,
and alert awareness.

RUTH HALEY BARTON

Always Secure in Our Gifts

In his grace, God has given us different gifts for doing certain things well.

ROMANS 12:6 NLT

Whether or not you hold higher degrees of education or years of experience, you will eventually find yourself in the company of someone by whom you feel dwarfed in terms of intellect or ability. Some people respond to this feeling by overreaching, attempting to cover for their insufficiency with lofty words or arrogance, though the cover-up never works. Others seem to flounder, losing their nerve completely, failing to operate even at their normal capacity. And still others seethe with envy and resentment, wasting precious energy on unproductive emotions.

It's likely that the problem is a simple misunderstanding. We may fail to realize that God grants to each of us certain strengths that resonate with His eternal purposes for our lives. Rather than feeling inferior or insecure, we should rejoice in the gifts of others, realizing that in truth we are simply different—what we lack in one area, we make up for in another. It isn't about one person being better, but rather God's deep desire that we realize our need for each other.

Don't hesitate to admire someone for the gifts God has given. Doing so does not diminish you in any way. As you spend time alone with God, your own special gifts and abilities will shine forth.

Light for your path

John 13:34
Romans 12:9–10
1 Corinthians 12:4–11; 13:4–8
Ephesians 4:31–32
Philippians 2:2–4
1 Thessalonians 5:11
1 Peter 4:8

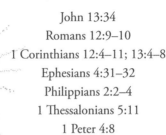

*Pick up a yardstick to measure
your life against anyone else's,
and you've just picked up a stick
and beaten up your own soul.*

ANN VOSKAMP

1/9

All by Design

*Known unto God are all his works
from the beginning of the world.*

ACTS 15:18 KJV

*S*erendipity explains those chance meetings that blossom into a vibrant friendship; those happy accidents that spark a routine day with unanticipated joy; those coincidences so good that they seem the stuff of fiction. By contrast, the word *design* describes a planned event or something prepared ahead of time.

Those two words, opposite in meaning, come together in God's wisdom. Blessings you never could have expected come into your life seemingly by chance, but each one has been in God's mind for you from the beginning. Fantastic news arrives as if out of the blue, yet God, in His divine knowledge, has been planning it all along. Your serendipity has always been His design for you.

Think about the many times serendipity has blessed, brightened, and changed your life. Can you perceive God's design behind it all? Can you look back and see His fingerprint on your life?

Maybe later today, your warm smile, caring touch, or encouraging words will lift the heart of someone you just happen to meet. Serendipity? It's being designed right now by God's Spirit at work in you!

Light for your path

Genesis 39:3
Job 23:14
Proverbs 16:9
Isaiah 14:27
Daniel 4:34–35
Romans 8:28, 38–39
2 Peter 1:3

Hope comes from knowing I have
a sovereign, loving God
who is in every event in my life.

LISA BEAMER

God may be invisible, but He's in touch.
You may not be able to see Him, but He is in control....
That includes all of life—past, present, future.

CHARLES SWINDOLL

Generosity of Spirit

> *He who sows sparingly will also reap sparingly, and he who sows bountifully will also reap bountifully.*
>
> 2 CORINTHIANS 9:6 NKJV

Generosity is a quality that everyone seems to admire. Some people may not understand it ("Why would she give so much money to that charity?"), but still, few people would find any real fault with those who give generously to others.

You don't need a huge bank account or an embarrassment of riches to be a generous giver. Generosity takes many forms, some of which have nothing to do with finances. When you are alone with God, ask Him to show you how you can become generous; He may show you that you already are. Do you volunteer with a charity? Do you listen compassionately to your friends when they're pouring out their hearts to you? Do you share encouragement from God's Word with someone who needs it? In short, do you give of your time, talents, and energy even when it's inconvenient to do so?

That's generosity of spirit, and just about everyone can have it—including those who are homebound but spend their time in prayer for others, and those who have little but share what they have with those who have less. By cultivating a generous spirit, you discover even more ways you can enrich the lives of others. And as you reflect God's Spirit of love, you'll be drawn closer to Him.

Light for your path

Leviticus 27:30–32
Deuteronomy 15:7–11
Proverbs 3:9–10; 21:13
Malachi 3:10
Matthew 6:1–4; 25:40
Luke 6:38
Acts 2:44–45; 4:32–37; 20:35
Romans 12:10, 13
2 Corinthians 9:6–12
Ephesians 5:20
James 2:15–16
1 John 3:17–18

Give yourself entirely to those around you....
A kind gesture can reach a wound
that only compassion can heal.

STEVE MARABOLI

Putting the Bible First

*Remember what Christ taught,
and let his words enrich your lives
and make you wise.*

COLOSSIANS 3:16 TLB

In Psalm 119, there are three verses that help us figure out whether the Bible is as important to us as it should be. Verse 72 says, "The law from your mouth is more precious to me than thousands of pieces of silver and gold" (NIV). Is God's Word more important to you than money—even big stacks of it?

Verse 103 says, "How sweet are your words to my taste, sweeter than honey to my mouth!" (NIV). Is the Bible more important to you than food?

Verse 148 reads, "My eyes stay open through the watches of the night, that I may meditate on your promises" (NIV). Is God's Word more important to you than sleep?

When our lives prove that the Bible holds more value to us than money, food, or sleep, we know it is dwelling in us richly, changing our lives and lighting our path.

When was the last time you deliberately chose God's Word over money, food, or sleep? Make room in your schedule in order to have more time to read your Bible. Before long, you will fall in love with God's Word and start reading it because you want to!

Light for your path

Psalm 119
Isaiah 40:8
Luke 11:28
Colossians 3:16–17
2 Timothy 3:16–17
Hebrews 4:12
James 1:22

Like waifs clustered around a blazing fire,
we gathered around [the Bible],
holding out our hearts to its warmth
and light. The blacker the night
around us grew, the brighter and truer...
burned the Word of God.

CORRIE TEN BOOM

Giving Our Best

Whatever you do, work at it with
all your heart, as working for the Lord,
not for human masters.

COLOSSIANS 3:23 NIV

Striving for excellence is different from promoting perfectionism. After all, only God is perfect. For Him, excellence is synonymous with perfection. For the rest of us, excellence means doing our very best, even if our best means making a few mistakes along the way.

Excellence begins with an attitude that says, "I'll do this job as if I were doing it for God Himself." Imagine how that would change even the minor jobs before you today. If you were preparing breakfast for Jesus, making His bed, attending to a project He put in your in-box, wouldn't each task be done to the very best of your ability?

In actuality, everything you do is a thank-You gift to the One who created you. You alone determine the quality of the gift you give. Again, God isn't asking for perfection. He's simply asking you to put your heart into everything you do. When you do, you receive more than you give. Enthusiasm, joy, accomplishment, fulfillment…the gifts keep accumulating when you live life with excellence and heart.

Light for your path

Numbers 27:2–4
Joshua 24:15
1 Chronicles 28:20
2 Chronicles 2:1
Ecclesiastes 8:1
Acts 4:29–31
Philippians 3:13–14

Strive for excellence, not perfection.

H. JACKSON BROWN JR.

*What is the distance between someone
who achieves their goals consistently
and those who spend their lives
and careers merely following?
The extra mile.*

GARY RYAN BLAIR

All Scripture is inspired by God
and is useful to teach us what is
true and to make us realize
what is wrong in our lives.
It corrects us when we are wrong
and teaches us to do what is right.

2 TIMOTHY 3:16 NLT

Words of Life

For the word of God is alive and powerful. It is sharper than the sharpest two-edged sword, cutting between soul and spirit, between joint and marrow. It exposes our innermost thoughts and desires.

HEBREWS 4:12 NLT

Some people have the perception that God's Word is a book of rules for the religious, something similar to an employee handbook at a corporation. Others perceive it to be a compilation of wise sayings and timely truths, comparable to the works of ancient Greek philosophers. And still others believe it to be a storybook full of charming fairy tales and whimsical anecdotes.

As a whole, the Scriptures comprise a variety of literary genres, composed over a vast span of history by a diverse group of writers. But the most amazing thing about the Word of God is its unique capacity to reach deeply into the hearts of its readers with profound relevance. It is the living Word.

The words of this book are not merely stored in your brain as data ready to be retrieved. They are words that enter into your mind and heart with the power to transform your perceptions, your decisions, your principles, your relationships, and your will. These words can search out and reveal your hidden motives. They find their way into the secret places of your heart, giving counsel in wisdom, bringing healing to your wounds, whispering hope in your despair, and lending courage in the face of your fears.

Light for your path

Proverbs 4:20–22; 30:5–6
Isaiah 55:10–11
John 5:39; 12:48–50
2 Timothy 3:16–17
2 Peter 1:20–21
Revelation 22:18–19

The gift of God is eternal life, spiritual life, abundant life through faith in Jesus Christ, the Living Word of God.

Anne Graham Lotz

Your Mission

Be holy in all you do.
1 PETER 1:15 NIV

"What's God want from me?" Have you ever asked that question? It's a great question—one you should be asking all the time. Peter gives you a bunch of answers to that question. This is your mission, should you choose to accept it (are you ready for this?): Praise God, put your hope in Him, be self-controlled, obedient, holy, submissive, and respectful. Don't pound on someone when they pound on you. Suffer for God, treat your friends (and your family!) as you would treat Christ Himself. And live in peace with everyone, be compassionate, sympathetic, and love everyone. Sound easy? Probably not.

The truth is, being a Christian can be really tough. In fact, there's a zero percent chance that you'll pull it off all by yourself. That's where the Holy Spirit giving you God's power comes in. But this list that Peter presents gives you a good idea of some of the things that will mark you as a Christ-follower. And it all starts with giving God the credit for everything. That is the beginning of being holy. To be holy means to be worthy of praise, to be working toward goodness and righteousness in every aspect of your life. Have you ever thought of yourself as holy? Accept the mission and start today.

Light for your path

Romans 12:1
2 Corinthians 7:1
Ephesians 5:3
2 Timothy 1:9
Hebrews 12:14
1 Peter 1:15–16

Our progress in holiness depends on God and ourselves—on God's grace and on our will to be holy.

MOTHER TERESA

You, a Conqueror

*Every child of God can obey him,
defeating sin and evil pleasure
by trusting Christ to help him.*

What's your image of a conqueror? History buffs may think of someone like Alexander the Great, who conquered much of the known world of his time, or Attila the Hun, who subdued most of Europe in the fifth century AD. But you, too, can be a conqueror—not by ruthlessly taking over a geographical area, but by relentlessly warring against the spiritual forces that try to bring you down. Those forces take many forms: the devastating effects of a drug culture that continually tries to entice your children to join in its addictions, the hidden habits of your own heart that tempt you to deny your marriage vows, the unforgiveness that prevents you from living a joyful life in God's presence.

The good news, however, is that God has given you everything you need to overcome whatever the world throws your way. That "everything" is Jesus Christ and your faith in Him. The faith that conquers the world—those spiritual forces that oppose you—is simply an abiding trust that God will do what He has said He will do. Take God at His word. His power working in and through you is all you need to become the conqueror He said you can be.

Light for your path

Matthew 17:20
Mark 11:22–26
Romans 1:17; 3:21–28; 4:3–5;
5:1–2; 10:8–11, 17
Ephesians 2:8–9
Hebrews 11:1–6; 12:2
1 Peter 1:6–9
1 John 5:4

When we pray for the Spirit's help…
we will simply fall down
at the Lord's feet in our weakness.
There we will find the victory and power
that come from His love.

ANDREW MURRAY

Never Giving Up

Be merciful to those who doubt.

JUDE 22 NIV

I had a friend who used to say some really awful things about Jesus. He'd make fun of Christians and laugh at God. He'd make me so angry, I'd want to hit him or worse. These verses remind me that a person who makes fun of God or has doubts about God needs to know the truth. Sometimes they are simply ignorant about God and His Word. When I got angry at my friend about his feelings toward God, I wasn't helping him get to know God; I was just making the situation worse. I wish I had tried to tell my friend the truth about God instead of getting angry at him. I regret not talking to him about his feelings. After all, Jesus had mercy on people who laughed at Him. He set the example for me to follow.

God still loves people who doubt Him. God never gives up on anyone. His mercies are new every morning—for all of us. Do you know someone who has doubts about God? Or dismisses the Bible as myth or fiction? Maybe you can talk to that person about those doubts and skepticism. Then ask your pastor or a trusted mentor to help you find some answers for your friend. And ask God to make you more patient with people who have doubts. Never give up. Everyone deserves mercy.

Light for your path

Isaiah 30:18
Matthew 6:14; 9:13
Ephesians 2:4–5
Jude 17–24

*God's mercy is so great that you may
sooner drain the sea of its water,
or deprive the sun of its light,
or make space too narrow,
than diminish the great mercy of God.*

CHARLES SPURGEON

1/17

Alpha and Omega

His eyes were like flames,
and on his head were many crowns.
REVELATION 19:12 TLB

In the Greek language (which is the language people spoke where this part of the Bible was written), the first letter of the alphabet was *alpha* and the last letter was *omega*. When Jesus says, "I am the Alpha and the Omega," He is saying that He is the beginning and the end (Revelation 1:8). In English, He might have said, "I am the A and the Z." This was especially important because this book deals with end-of-the-world stuff, and Jesus wanted us to understand that He will still be in charge when that happens.

Think of the Jesus you got to know in the stories of His years on earth. He was a simple carpenter, walking wherever He went, hanging out with poor people, and, in the end, nailed to an ugly cross. In these verses from Revelation, He's back where He came from—in heaven and in charge. The One on the white horse with fire in His eyes and crowns on His head—that's your friend, Jesus. He promises He's coming to take you to heaven someday soon. He was there at the beginning, and He will be there with you at the end. Can you think of anything more awesome?

Matthew 24:30
John 14:1–3
1 Thessalonians 4:16–17
Hebrews 9:28
Revelation 19:11–16; 22:12

As the first cause of all that exists,
Jesus cannot be limited
by the word Alpha. And as the Omega,
He is not the "end" as we know it.
He will continue to exist
into the everlasting,
never-ending future.

DAVE BRANON

The End, a New Beginning

I saw a new heaven and a new earth.
REVELATION 21:1 KJV

Beginning a book by reading the final chapter takes away the suspense. Once you know that the heroine is rescued, that the hero survives, and that their love for each other blossoms into the "happily ever after," what's the point of reading the rest of the story? Yet that's exactly what God invites you to do. He's given you the final chapter of this life in the book of Revelation. This final book in the Bible assures you that Jesus will return, that you will be rescued, and that your love for each other will grow throughout eternity. Knowing the end of this story isn't a "spoiler." It's a comfort.

The Bible doesn't spell out what's going to happen today. Today everything may go exactly the way you've pictured in your mind. Or an unexpected story line might take you in a direction you never dreamed you'd go. Regardless of what today holds, you know how the story ends. That means you can trade fear and worry for confidence and peace. Best of all, after the final chapter, an even more wonderful Part II begins.

Light for your path

John 3:16; 4:14; 6:47;
10:27–28; 11:25–26
Romans 6:22–23
Galatians 6:8
Titus 1:2
1 John 2:25; 5:11–13, 20

*The Bible could be trusted just as much
as if God had taken the pen
and written the words Himself.*

JOHN F. WALVOORD

*It ought to be placed in the forefront of all
Christian teaching that Christ's mission on earth
was to give men Life. "I am come," He said,
"that ye might have Life, and that ye
might have it more abundantly."*

HENRY DRUMMOND

If we will commit our ways
unto the Lord and trust Him,

He has promised that
He would direct our paths.

DEBRA AIKEN